Seal up the Thunder

Seal up the Thunder

Erin Noteboom

Then the seven thunders spoke. I was about to write,
but a voice came out of heaven, saying,
seal up what the thunder has said,
and do not write it down.
— Revelations 10

Wolsak and Wynn . Toronto

Cover image: "Mary Magdalene" © 1990 Robert Lentz
Author's photograph: Dr. Marguerite Tonjes
Typeset in Garamond, printed in Canada by The Coach House Printing Company, Toronto, Ontario

The publishers gratefully acknowledge the financial support of the Government of Canada through the BookPublishing Industry Development Program (BPIDP)for our publishing activities, as well as the support of the Canada Council for the Arts, and the Ontario Arts Council

The Canada Council | Le Conseil des Arts
for the Arts | du Canada

Canadian   Patrimoine
Heritage   canadien

ONTARIO ARTS COUNCIL
CONSEIL DES ARTS DE L'ONTARIO

Wolsak and Wynn Publishers Ltd
196 Spadina Avenue, Suite 303
Toronto, ON
Canada M5T 2C2

Library and Archives Canada Cataloguing in Publication

Noteboom, Erin, 1972-
    Seal up the Thunder / Erin Noteboom.

Poems
ISBN 0-894987-00-4

Title.

PS8577.0075S43 2005   C811'.6   C2004-907479

I am my beloved's and my beloved is mine

for my husband, James Bow

Contents

Revelation

Listen: I am going to tell you something.
You will not repeat it. You will be lucky
even to survive. When I speak,
your heart will catch like a match. When I speak
your pulse will turn to a tide. When I speak your ears
will hold all human words, like a wood full of birds,
they cry *lonely, lonely*. When you hear, your back
will arch like sky. You will call like the thunder:
bones, come together. Bones, take your order.

Be still. Your words are husk
for breath. They cannot make
the stones bleed water, or set the sun
ablaze past colour. I am the word
that made the clay curl up in fingers.
How can you answer? Be still
and I will make an oak of you. Be still
and I will put a bolt through you
and turn your lungs to hands
of lightning.
                    Do not be frightened.
You have wanted – wings. An end
to death. (Remember, I have walked
as pulse and skin. I know
what you long for.) Be still
and I will turn your ribs to wings,
your breastbone to the keel
of a bird: a deep cord
to anchor silence. Come, open
your mouth. I will put my book
on your tongue: a stone, a word, a wafer.
Become salt. Savour.

FIRST TESTAMENT

Suffrage to water

Oh water, that warms us
and dissolves us, oh medium
of our chemistry, oh breaker
of our bonds, oh drowner, oh sac
of life, oh maker of borders, oh grinder
of stone, oh thunderstorm,
oh frost, oh falls, oh storm surge —
spare us. From the slosh
of the jug, spare us. From the sting
of salt, spare us. From the lonely hish
of traffic, spare us. From hail,
from ice, from wave, spare us.
From the dredging of lakes,
from the grinning lip
of the well, from losing our names
like river in ocean, water,
spare us. We praise you, water,
your weathering patience,
your thickness in lungs,
your wholeness in drops, your selfless
displacement, your ceaseless swing
of sea. We praise you, water.
Source and mouth, we praise you.
Remember us, water.
Well and pump, remember us,
blood and lymph, remember us,
flood and dam, remember us,
comet and icecap, remember us.
Remember us, water, oh maker,
oh changer, oh restless, oh universal
solvent, oh born
in burning, oh breath
of stars, oh fine
and swirling
snow.

Cain reflects on cutting Abel's throat

Now I have lived a long time
and had not thought to see
something new – but something flew
(like sparrows flushed from roost
and then the tree is still)
something flew up, a rush
as fast as flame – and irrevocable.
He said just one word –
God – and it was like
my name. (Ah this
is what God likes –
the blood and flame.)
Your brother's blood
makes mouth in earth, God said
and with earth and blood
He marked me – half god,
half man, His at last,
and blushing –

After the flood

How quick the insects bred. For years,
after the greater beasts had struck out
for the blue and distant ridge, we saw
little else. Gnats rose up like sea smoke
from the muck, and grasshoppers
stripped the fireweed and kudzu, ate even
the dyed stripes of laundry, till we were left
with white tatters like signal flags,
limp on the bug-thick line.
It was years before the swallows
caught up to them. Crawling
years. Every night my Noah
went down to where the stone beach
slowly widened. He was remembering
the animals, their heads above
the sluggish waves, the stirred brown wake
of their leaving – the lion, snake-maned,
leading, the trundling hippo, the giraffe's
foolish neck sticking up
like a great sea serpent. He thought
they might come back, you see –
Japheth and Shem, oaring the little boat.
A horse, perhaps. At least
the dog. In later years,
he took to gathering stones,
handing them to me smooth from the sea
and stinking. No matter how I washed them,
they always smelled of flood. I know
why he did it, though. The water
made them lovely, awash
in radiance, a jumbled rainbow
in the bottom of the bowl.

How even the holy cover their faces

Then Abraham reached out his hand and took the knife to kill his son. But the angel called to him from heaven, and said, "Abraham, Abraham!" And he said, "Here I am." And he said, "Do not lay your hand on the boy or do anything to him; for now I know that you fear God, since you have not withheld your son, your only son, from me." And Abraham looked up and saw a ram, caught in a thicket by its horns. Abraham went and took the ram and offered it up as a burnt offering instead of his son.
— Genesis 22

Deanna Laney, called by God, gave up her children.
This is not a story. Testimony:

How she woke near midnight
and took the oldest first onto the lawn,
how the sprinklers came on, how they ran
to the rock garden.
How she had decided on stones.

How the Lord put a stone at her feet as a sign,
how she put a stone in the crib
as a sign. How a baby's head fills the hand
like a stone, how sleep fills it with heavy
decision. How she woke near midnight
with her heart filled up and heard: *it's time,*
it's time —

How she heard it first
when the baby squeezed a frog,
how gold its eyes bugged out
clear as a message. How he toddled to her,
stone in chubby offering. How his name
was Aaron. How her boys were Joshua, Luke,
and Aaron.

If the ministry of death, says the Word, *came in glory,*
how much more, then ... How God sent the ram.
How *you can't see why,* she testifies. *You've just*
got to. How in scripture, they say
Here I am.

How her boys were Joshua, Luke, and Aaron.
How she took the oldest first
into the garden, how she smashed,
how she pulled the body by beloved feet
into bushes. How she looked
for the ram. How her robe
and white pyjamas.
How her wet feet
and hands.

Leah names her sons

I knew I was marrying bitterness –
knew he wouldn't want me, soft-eyed,
too old. For my sister's sake
he rolled the boulder from the well,
her sheep he watered, her throat
he kissed. My father demanded
seven years' service as a bridal price
and filled my mouth with stones
when I would deny his plan:
a night-wedding, a heavy veil,
and Jacob, seven years pent, too hasty
even to spare a kiss. He took me
in darkness and joy and called me
Rachel, Rachel.
                          And I answered.
Of course, I did. I knew I'd get
one night's tenderness, one dawn's
sleepy smile before that look
of stunned despising. He spent
a second seven years my father's shepherd
to get Rachel. Slept out with the flock
most nights, or came in, manure
matting his hair, his back as hard
as baked clay, his thrusts
brutal. I bore him sons,

and named them
          see, a son
named them
          prayer answered
named them
          my husband love me.

But he did not soften, went always
to Rachel, by then sister-wife, her womb
empty as a dried-up well. My boys.

I named them
   sing praise
named them
   just reward
named them
   my husband exalt me.

Jacob, you found in me
a salted country, a line of bitterness.
The old gods grant to women –
too old, weak-eyed – a witchy power.
I would use it, Rachel, to put your children
down wells, to set a stone
in your womb, to name you
mother of weeping, name you
comfortless. And father,
night-bargainer, slave-maker, a stone
on your tongue, dust for your thirst,
and the border of my country,
stones, stones, stones.

Moses: Curled in a hand of earth

*[The Lord said to Moses], "I Myself will make all My Glory pass before
you, and will proclaim My Name before you, and be gracious to you.... But
you cannot see My face, for it would be death to you." And He said:
"Behold, there is a place by Me, and you shall stand there on the rock, and
while My glory is passing by, I will put you in the cleft of the rock and
cover you with My hand until I have passed by."*

— from Exodus 33

Curled in a hand of earth and covered
by something like a wing,
Moses felt the heart within him
like the Red Sea split
and trembling, and in that moment strangely
he remembered Miriam, her face lifting
even as the basket reeds
grew damp —

Moses: On the mountaintop

According to tradition, Moses died of the kiss of God,
and God himself buried him.

At first a sign, as if He were
a common sorcerer: a tree
untouched by fire. But then He called me:
Moses, Moses, and I heard, *My Foundling Prince,*
Beloved Murderer. He knew me.
He unstopped me
like a jar.

Of course, I argued: "I'm fool, I stammer – "
I will turn your stutter-tongue
to living fire. Put plagues in your hands.
Give you power.

But now
it's been so long.
My heart's a flute.
My feet are dry as any viper.
Show me the honey-place but do not take me
any further – My Life Itself, My Living God,
Beloved Murderer.

Delilah, on contradictions

[Delilah said to Sampson], "How can you say, 'I love you,' when your heart is not with me? You have deceived me these three times and have not told me where your great strength is." .... So he told her all that was in his heart and said to her,".... If I am shaved, then my strength will go from me – I will become weak and be like any other man."

– from Judges 16

He burned my country
and I loved him. I betrayed him
and he stayed. He killed my brothers
and I held him. I betrayed him
and he stayed. What's between us
I can't tell you – musk and lust,
a lion's skin – dark mane tangled
with the tawny, blood and honey
on the wind. I cut his hair
because he told me, I loved him soft,
I loved him hard – so I broke him
with a razor, wove his hair
into my heart.

Sarah of the seven grooms

*[Tobiah said to Raphael], "... I have been told that she has already been
given in marriage seven times, and that each time her bridegroom has died
in the bridal room. They say it is a demon that loves her, and I am afraid."*
— Book of Tobit

They say it is a demon, takes my grooms. I don't
deny it. Gossips raise their hands to hide
their whispers. Merchants thrust out glossy dates,
red jars of greenest oil for my hair. Black, it flashes,
and proud men duck their eyes. And it may be
a demon. I know that something curls
with me, neither snake nor smoke, but a twist
like quick water. It shines. It smells
of storms. The men smell it, as they edge
into the bridal room. They are afraid, then,
of a small woman perched
on the cot's edge. My mother folds
the bridal price in linen. Outside the window,
my father digs, his spade chuckling. The groom
uncovers my hair. The power wells
and rises. Seven times now. A holy number.

No one will touch me. After years,
a stranger comes, a kinsman, his heart
beating hard, an angel beside him
whispering spells. Still, there is something
in his eyes I like: a worship
and a wariness.

Ezekiel and the bones

I came then to the bone plain,
bones hollowed and heaped and dry, so dry,
the sand hissed against them
with a sound like cymbals.
Prophesy, cried the angel. What
could I say? I stuttered: *Listen, listen.*
Elohim crouched like storm cloud,
uncovered His face and cried aloud.
It hollowed me. I thought the world
had lost all sound. But then – a click
of pebbles falling, a patter
like a sudden rain. From the yellow plain
a choking dust rose up, and the jumble shuddered
as a mare shakes to free herself from fleas.
A voice, then: mouthless, throatless,
roaring like the sea. Elohim stopped
my ears. *The dead may speak*
with tongues you should not hear,
He said. *They may accuse me.*

PSALMS

Yours is the day

Yours is the day, Lord, and yours the night,
the stale end of winter, sky like wet newspaper.
Yours the disputed city, the woman with her arm flung
running for the water. Yours the morning news.
Lord, you split the waters to our need, you set the stars
on wheels. You get up before dawn, feed the cat
and grind the coffee. You read all the mail.
For you it is always morning, the day opening.
Oh I need so much from you. The dust is getting grimy,
there are ten loads of laundry. No poems will come
except this one, and I feel silly. I have bills to pay
and not much money, though I have never been hungry.
Yours, Lord, is the discount grocery, the day-old bread,
half-soft peppers, and all my neighbours: the woman in the blue chador
who doesn't want my prayers. Yours Lord are winter apples, onions,
and especially potatoes. Everything is yours – aspirin, arthritis,
the ache of late winter, the fearless crocus. What does that teach us?
For I am not fearless. I sit through the day at my desk
swamped in nothing, not writing, twisting and hopeless, and the rain
turns to sleet, then snow. The whole world slowly changes
until it's beautiful. I put on Miles Davis and you
are the pause, the empty note, the hanging silence.
Lord, remember the dove of your people. I am caught
and throwing myself against the window and I want to be
a sparrow, my wings in your hand, and the door opening –

ॐ
Psalm 74

in the tilling of the land the Lord is

In the tilling of the land the Lord is

the plow that takes the rabbit
                    and the rabbit
the breaking earth in curls and clods

He lies in the furrows
they grow sweet with shadow

The blessing of the Lord broods over the fields
and the fields blossom

Abundance like a cloth woven loosely
drapes the field corn
embroidered pasture   goldenrod & wild carrot
beaded with cattle

Let the hills sing
Let the blades swing
Let the threshers come home in the evening
            blistered and singing

~✤~
Psalm 65

after a loss, I have walked long in silence
I have walked long in silence, scuffing my shoes

The Lord shall come down
       like rain on the grasses
like rain before mowing
the Lord shall come down

His name falls alike
       on the wheat and the thistle
His scythe takes alike
       the grain and the weeds

The rain comes in August
       while hay is still sweetening
a sweetness of rot
       the wet windrowed fields

His pitiless comfort
       like the dew in the morning
my heart is soaked through –
       I am done with this singing

༄
Psalm 72

scraps and velvet

Lord, you wither me

My body scorched
like August grass
My mind less

even than that –
a wind in the grass
　　　　one cloud passing

And you – Endless,
you wear the ocean as a scarf,
the wind as a ribbon in your hair

The earth wears out
and you change it like an apron
like a quilt you shake
the embroidered stars

Endless, my days are short –
Do not cut them

God of silks and scraps
of selvage and velvet
let me lean at your knees
as you hum over piecework

My God of the ragbag
with the needle in your mouth –

꙾

Psalm 102

but I have stilled and quieted

But I have burned to the waterline
But I have cried myself like a child to sleep
But I have stilled and quieted my soul

What is this –
       destroyed hope
       content despair

– too wonderful for me
Like a swaddled child, my soul within me
Like milk faith fills my belly

And I purr like that cat – remember? –
orange fur in my lap
all torn by the auger

Psalm 131

**let my prayer be set forth in your sight as incense
the lifting up of my hands as the evening sacrifice**

grey and greased dishwater
late, last thing – the whole day
and nothing consecrated

slouched in dullness
couch crumbed, mindless TV
& even sleep held under
a skim of chemicals

sleep your great benediction
the body fills
          with liquid heavy
a moon pull – honey or oil – prayer
as a kind of drowsing

from the fry pan
I lift my hands
          dripping like hyssop

꧅

Psalm 141

there is an oracle in my heart

there is an oracle in my heart
        a pool reflecting

poisonous I am poisoned
proud am paralysed
timid, shut
        in trembling

like a little lake holding mountains
my heart holds – Oh

I am too little for this, Lord,
let me
come into your house

like a child
taking off my shoes

ৡৢ
Psalm 36

like a stranger I have stood by the world amazed

The sun comes up
      in its glory of physics
and goes down
      in its glory of physics

and every day I doubt you.

Oh God I have been silly.
I have heard voices
and listened. I have fought
and lost and raged
at occupation. I may simply be crazy.

Like a stranger I have stood by the world amazed.
I have numbered the forces and loved
the fern curls of particles
and everything elegant delicate
charged and spinning –

The law that bends the light
of stars – is that
yours? This crooked heart
broken world –

Nothing has chosen me
Nothing calls
and I answer

it cuts my eyes
and so unblinded circumcised
I stand a stranger
               amazed and seeing –

there is no reason
for the locust in fall to turn
     so yellow
or let the smallest wind
spin down, leaf by leaf

    its trust, its breath, its blessing

Psalm 119

**let us worship the Lord in the beauty of holiness
let all the earth tremble before him**

this scrap patch under the power line –
     thistle, broom, and side-oats
     quaking aspen and milkweed empty-handed
in early snow –

how it muffles and sharpens
sweetens the silence

the pylon to a spire

in the snow a cricket sings
with his whole body
with his only, holy body

the buffalo grass
     softly burdened
bows its seed heads

in cold the cricket folds up
his black vestments

꙾

Psalm 96

so the heart in her indigo

as the sea holds the water
so the Lord holds the earth

it is his temple
and the gate of his temple

it is his joy
and the fount of his joy

as the world waits for dawn
so the heart in her indigo

so the heart in her bride-dress
longing and listening

I am awake, Lord
let something start singing

༈

Habukkuk, Chapters 1 & 2

as the foxglove loves the fur of the bee

for my husband, James

As the foxglove loves the fur of the bee
flushed and spotted, long-throated
with longing, let me
smear your face with pollen,
take fur inside me
mouth and belly – oh
it's been too long,
the sun has swung
and all my dews are gone, but
only bid me and I'll open
like a rock-spring, I'll bloom like a wadi,
only touch me and I'm milk
and honey, your rose of Sharon,
your stargazer lily

Song of Solomon

oh the gates

mason jars, quick pickles   chairs countertops
the light that loves the bowls of spoons

oh the gates of heaven

holsteins impossibly
hay sweet
cottonwood tossing
chicory & clover   each fingered blossom

oh the gates

cirrus cumulus cumulostratus   starlings
river-stones   sheets & sweet skin tang *oh*

the gates of heaven
         are everywhere

               motes in the slant: squint
and they open

WISDOM WRITINGS

Heart-cuckoo God

Heart-cuckoo God
we feed him our worms and he grows
monstrous – false thing, God
of the parasite wasps. I think I made you.
I think I spun you Sugar
– my whirlwind mind.
It is possible.
I admit it is at least
possible.

The world is thick
as caterpillar tents. For anything you like,
there's evidence. The world is beautiful.
The world is monstrous.

Pain takes me
with his axe to the head.
I cry out
and like a lover he
takes me again. If I beg

what answers? Heart's cuckoo,
I think I made you.
I think I coaxed and called you
till you purred round my shins
like a stray.

De profundis

All night, Oh God, you hold my eyes
open

My thoughts crawl
churning and curdling

sick as the sea

At 3 AM
I call to you
From the heaped sink
I call to you
Sticky and swarming
I call to you

Oh God, here I am
having bad sex
Here I am
on a blank road
Here I am
with a shut heart
Here I am
listening

§

By a pillbox, one soldier leans
The sky is heavy and stirring
The sea is heavy and stirring

No light for his night watch
No words in the salt crash
Time clots like an old wound
like a beast of shadow
But he stands
listening, listening

§

Lord, break the world
in lightning, let the thunder sing
Let the rim of air turn hard
and rain with arrows

Let them say – *Look*
where He walks on the water
Look – a door in the sea

End this night
in violence
suddenly

Or draw me to you
like the dawn
rose and silent

❧
Psalm 77, Psalm 130

Job's plea

My God moves mountains
       though they are faithless

He brings the earthquake
       and walks on the sea

At His word the sun stops
       the stars stand there trembling

Yet He slips by me
       soft as the Spring

How shall I plead
       with the Master of Monsters

When my God strikes against me
       again and again

When He strikes like a hawk
       and no one can stop Him

When even one breath
       is too much to ask

How shall I plead
       what court is great enough

How can I stand
       to His crushing word

My innocence no shelter
       against such a power

If indeed I am innocent
       how can I be sure?

Oh Wisdom, this world

Who has mapped every grain of the shore?
Who has cupped the wind in hands?
Who has wrapped the waters in robes?

Not me. Nothing holy moves my tongue.
I have been a fool over and over.
Yet I say this —

Three things cannot be satisfied:

> *the barren womb*
> *the sword, always hungry*
> *the fire that never says enough*

Three things cannot be finished:

> *the sea fills with rivers*
> *yet does not rise*
> *the eye fills with light*
> *yet is always looking*
> *the ground fills with names*
> *yet does not speak*

Three things pass understanding:

> *how eagles see*
> *the clear wheels of air*
> *how the iron*
> *knows north*
> *how marriage moves*
> *between a man and a woman*

Oh Wisdom, this world
is too wonderful for me.

If my heart falters,
let it stop. If my eyes lie
cut them out. If I am foolish,
cover my mouth. Then lift me,
light me, bring me
to life. Give me joy, give me
love in this world. Help me as I stagger.
Hold me as I sleep.

≈

Proverbs 30

Chalcedony, chrysoprase, lapis, onyx

The wall was made of jasper, and the city of pure gold, as pure as glass.
the foundations of the city walls of every kind of precious stone. The first
foundation was jasper, the second sapphire, the third chalcedony, the fourth
emerald, the fifth sardonyx, the sixth carnelian, the seventh chrysolite, the
eight beryl, the ninth topaz, the tenth chrysoprase, the eleventh jacinth, and
the twelfth amethyst. The twelve gates were twelve pearls, each gate made of
a single pearl. The great street of the city was of pure gold, like transparent
glass. I did not see a temple in the city, because the Lord Himself and the
Lamp are its temple. — Revelation 21

Chalcedony, chrysoprase, lapis, onyx:
the great bowl of the St Lawrence
changes – water in the net of its surface
is first deeper than twilight then softer
as the sky slides past it – the air deep blue
and the water blue-green and luminous.

Amethyst, serpentine, sapphire, sardonyx:
In the great vision, heaven is founded on five
and seven stones – imagine the seer
struck down in the gold bowl of dessert,
the sky flamed like heated copper.
Imagine that he wrote tasting honey,
his feet wet, wild bees in mouth and pockets.

Carnelian, topaz, bloodstone, jacinth:
We live beside a world of strangeness,
the bee world of blazoned roses.
Serpentine, emerald: It has no temple,
though doors slide into us. Jasper, jade:
the morning stands translated.
In a dream I walk down stairs.
I wake, and walk down stairs.

Book of Wisdom

I

By chance we are born
      and time leaves no trace of us

Our breath and words scatter
      like smoke in the wind

The spark of our reason
      goes out with our heartbeat

Our spirit is poured
      like air into air

Even our names
      will go like cloud shadows

And so we are foolish
      we make pacts with death

We seek a strong passing
      like the flight of an arrow

But the air heals behind us
      leaving no wound

As a hunter tracks birds
      so history remembers us

The blue sky a seal
      that closes our names

Broken we turn
      and grope for what's lasting

We dig in the ground
     you are common as onions

We go out at dawn
     you are there at the door

II

Our old gods were crooked
      scrap wood full of knots

We found in a stick
      eyes and strange faces

We daubed it with red
      and covered its blemishes

Nailed to a wall
      it does not even stand

Our old gods were hollow
      a potter's poor pinchings

From common muck
      we make jugs and idols

Our god's nose is shut
      its mouth holds no voices

Image of sorrow –
      of a child lost early

We touch its smooth palm
      but fingers don't grasp ours

Our poor mortal hands
      can make only dead things

Our bodies were clay
      and to clay they're going

Yet you breathe into us
      poor jars of ashes

With your breath in us
      we sing like bottles

III

Away from you Lord
     we are shut into trembling

Nothing gives light
     not fire, not stars

The least thing a terror
     the hissing of insects

Even the air
     that brushes our faces

The darkness grows
     a limitless prison

Vast as the underworld
     empty and trackless

We will never get out of it
     we are bound and sentenced

We are stricken with noises
     the hollow hills echoing

Then you crack the darkness
     you come bearing torches

You stand before us
     a pillar, a sunbeam

The true world is shining
     we blink and are dazzled

IV

To the violent you send us
    fierce but unarmoured

Though already the corpses
    have fallen in heaps

Though already the rivers
    are swarming with sorcery

The fish turned to frogs
    the honey to stinging

We overcome bitterness
    without strength or weapon

The glory of history
    stands ranked around us

The world's great shining
    wraps us like a robe

Then land creatures change
    taking to water

Then sea creatures change
    and walk over land

And death fills our bodies
    as melt fills the gold

As trees fill with stillness
    a stillness of birds

SECOND TESTAMENT

Bone Pastor

Bone pastor, panis vere,
Iesu, nostri miserere:
Tu nos pasce, nos tuere,
Tu nos bona fac videre
in terra viventium.
– St. Thomas Aquinas

Christ our bone pastor,
our bread, our wound,
Christ who told the women
weeping at the tomb
Do not hold me.
Christ the King
of thorns, of mustard seeds,
Lord of buttons, of palms
and donkeys, dust-caked
and thirsty. Emmanuel
with us in waves,
in dishes, in nails,
in the long drag
of water from the well,
our hands rough and shoulders
aching. Wonder counsellor,
Lord of the lopped-off hand,
the covered eye, Lord of dragonflies
and contradictions,
single-hearted Lord
of lions. Let us live
in our bodies until
we are buried, come to us
like phosphorus, burn us,
change.

Zachariah, Elizabeth, and John

1. Zachariah

*The angel said to him: your wife Elizabeth shall bear a son, whom you
shall name John. Joy and gladness will be yours, and many will rejoice at his
birth. Zachariah answered: how can this be? I am an old man, and my
wife is old.*   *— Gospel of Luke*

The angel struck me dumb
for doubt. How could I not
have doubted? Elizabeth –
after fifty years, I knew
every inch of her. Men called her
barren, as if she were
a salted field, but to me
she is not garden but temple,
more dear to me than the one I serve
as priest. To her, my heart
kneels, to her I bring the attar
and the oil: my Jerusalem, my pillar
of cedar, my ark of the tabernacle,
the wings of my heart that open
and close. I came to her, wordless
and radiant, and she knew
what I wanted.

Elizabeth

Mary set out in haste to the hill country, to a town in Judah, where she entered Zachariah's house and greeted Elizabeth. When Elizabeth heard the greeting, the baby leapt in her womb.   *— Gospel of Luke*

As she came running up the hill,
I thought she looked too young
to be married: barefoot, still,
her hair uncovered. I wondered,
too, what brought her here
in such a hurry. Not my news,
for I had shut myself away,
and kept it secret. And then
she called to me, and all at once,
I knew. The baby danced
within me, and my heart leapt
and lurched — how great
a joy! And she, so small.

John

A herald cries in the wilderness:
make ready the way of the Lord.
Clear him a straight path.
Every valley shall be filled
and every mountain and hill laid low.
                    – Gospel of Luke

There were days when I believed
it would happen: I'd speak
and the sand would begin to stir,
to pour, to fill the valley
as water fills a new-struck well.
I'd raise a hand and squint to see it start –
but it never did. I have seen
one miracle, and it wasn't
mine. I have only been
a voice. Though even a voice
can move the world.
That's my first memory: Mary spoke,
and my whole life opened,
though I was not yet born, and Mary
had no power of her own. My cell
is dark, now. Faint, a dancer's bells
drip in like rain.
                    A blameless death
will be one last heralding.

The sparrow child

This little child Jesus when he was five years old was playing at the ford of
a brook: and he gathered together the waters that flowed there into pools,
and made them straightway clean, and commanded them by his word alone.
And having made soft clay, he fashioned thereof twelve sparrows
                                              — Gospel of Thomas

Like any child, my boy seems now,
toddling in the clay beds, making sparrows
from mud, commanding the creek
to clear pools. Once, the scribe's son
stirred them with a stick. Jesus
raised a quick hand, and the lad
fell dead. Later, the scribe's wife
weeping, her boy limp across her lap.
Jesus said "He's only sleeping," and kissed,
and woke the lad from death
to sleep. "What is he," the mother stuttered,
"what?" I ran. I could not say – My son
and not my son. In his hands
a heavy sparrow stirs towards feathers.

Night litany

Our Lady of the late night hospital,
Lily of antiseptic, Queen of morphine drips,
I'm in so much pain.
White lady, help me.
Cool hands, make haste to help me.
Light of visions, Robe of roses,
I give you my skin.
Who squatted in a stable, swaddle me.
Who lost a child, lift me.
Who said yes, beyond
all reason, graciously –
graciously hear me.

Lady, the barest moon goes down
over the skyline, the sky
greens and deepens,
the moon like a pulled bow
and the milk-spattered sky.
Lady of shadows, Lady of ferns
stirring, Lady of owls,
stay with me. The hours
fold like linen and nurses
pad by on rounds. Seven-fold
hum of hospitals, drug-stranged
Star of dreams –
guide me.

Queen of refugees, this
is your place, cool Egypt
of blank halls and cinderblock.
Tent of oxygen, Lady of partitions,
Walled garden, hear me.
Who sobbed in darkness,
save me. Who carried swords,
make haste to save me.

I call on you, God
mother, powerful surrender –
watch over me.
I am stretched like a belly
but there's nothing in me.
Breathe over me. Lady.
Breathe over me.

The kingdom of God is within you

Gates, squares, market stalls,
wildcat dumps, full burn barrels of regret.
Potters turning kickwheels with their warped feet,
lovers in doorways, transvestite prostitutes,
rain on the roofs, libraries. Dovecotes, wild doves,
chickens, roosters, peacocks
in ornamental gardens. Zoos. Lions.
Storehouses of grain, of spices, oils,
children's hopes. Schools. Occupying forces
with dice cups. Women with yokes
and water jars, women with the full weight
on curved shoulders. And above this a hill
of crosses, clattering tombs.

It's an ordinary kingdom, from your gates of eye
and ivory to your heart's midden, secret springs.
But one city touches another
and the walls blink into saffron.
One city touches another and both ring
like trumpets. A king gives a beggar girl
a crown of rubies, peaches in heavy cream.

You are the king
and the beggar girl,
the beehives and the rain,
the dice and the soldiers, the well water,
the feet and shoulders
of the poor. You are the guard
flinging open the gates,
the horse of the royal messenger
that stamps like the heart, and prances.

Resurrection

The women (Mary Magdelene, Mary the mother of James, and Salome)
turned and fled from the tomb, seized with trembling and bewilderment.
– Gospel of Mark

As they ran their hands shook, oil sloshed
from jars and spice from fingers, and shadows
fled before them, cast by the angel,
and their teeth chattered. Birds swooped down
for seeds, sparrows and finches and graveyard mice
bright-eyed and wild. The path was rocky and Salome
ripped one sandal and her blood scattered
and sprang up in great branches, olive and myrtle,
dogwood in white blossom, until the hill was veiled
and bridal. The oil anointed stones with river-colour
until they made a river: first
a trickle, then braided runnels
like the inside of a wrist, and then
the mouth of the tomb became
the womb of rain.

The conversion of Paul

[Paul said], "When the blood of your martyr Stephen was shed, I stood
there giving my approval and guarding the clothes of those who were
killing him."   *— Acts 22:20*

You will remember that I watched you dying.
You were buried to the waist. Your hands were not flung up,
which puzzled me, though it may be they were broken.
You wore a crown of blood as if of ribbons.
The coats around me seemed to thicken.

Do you know they say you had the face
of an angel? I admit I never saw that, but there was something,
        in that last moment, when you tilted up
your chin — not wings, but a kind of brightness,
a door opening.

   Therefore when I fell
from the horse (my heart hinged, a hoof
nicked my ear) and heard a voice (a radiant pain
and blood ribboning), I said *Who*
and thought I would hear: *Stephen.*

Acta Thomae

The Acta Thomae, or Acts of Thomas, is an early Christian
account of the life and works of St. Thomas the Apostle.

The doubter. They were beginning to call him that,
forty days later, at the meeting where they divided up the world.
The descending ghost had brought him no great gifts.
Truth to tell, he hadn't seen those famous flames at all,
and in those tongues heard only babble.
Even in his own. But he knew better
than to say so twice and kept his silence.
Hoped that silence could become belief.

The meeting. They gave him India. India! He
whose opened mouth could only gabble
of the gift. How could he teach a strange
and foreign people? He refused. A vision came –
the dead friend who had been
in many visions. Who said blessed
are those who do not see him.
Blessed are those, not seeing him,
who sleep. Blessed was Peter, whose great fear
was thrice forgiven. Did they call him
the renouncer, call him cock-crow?
No. Blessed was Peter, who snored.

The vision told him go. His heart
told him he'd be a fool to go. A fool
who would make foolish this great
and fragile thing. He slipped out as the Lord
had slipped in, intending – what?   Suddenly,
a dropped burlap, wet-wheat smell, cosh to the head.

A woven, reeling darkness. No vision this, but real
as a rat in a sack. He woke sick
on a sailing barge. Christ our slavetaker
stood over him. Sold him to a man like a magus, servant
to a foreign king. In the prison hold he heard
the rats and rumour – India! We are sold
to India. He prayed: *My Lord, there's no mistaking this one –*
a thought the Acta Thomae makes: *Thy will be done.*

But it was seven days before he said that,
seven days seasick and starving. The king's strange servant
eyed him, asked him where he'd learned
the language. *A gift,* he said, *for languages.*
Like Daniel who could read the writing on the wall.
The king's man squinted. Asked to be told the story.
Thy will be done, the doubter thought,
and in a pouch secret as a wound in the side Thomas
found his purchase price. *The telling is hard,*
he began, *but here is a place to start.*

WORLD WITHOUT END

Henini

I am talking to the cat and this occurs
in that touch on my ear –
As we to beasts God speak

I hear my name and

Holy,
cries the cardinal
here here here here here

A book of hours

Dawn

Oh let us have an hour
for coming on, an hour
of light switches, a coffee hour,
an hour for inking pens,
a toothbrush hour, an hour of sight,
an hour of light deepening over
the banks of morning.

Work

The mind bunches its black shoulders
and flaps free of the body.
How serious the mind is!
Tilting its glossed head.
Marching stiff-legged in ditches.

Noon

The sun, marching.
Under that great eye,
nothing dares.
Even hills
pull in their shadows.

Progress

Great plumes from steel mills
and lakers in long lines –
how lovely even this
power line beaded with starlings.

Pinking

Tender as sepia the sun
slants into the hour
of things becoming themselves,
the leaves more leaves, your hands
more hands, our shingled roof
a lid of shining.

Long shadows

As a great wave into shallows rises,
so longing crests
on the shelf of the day

Moon

Between mirror and shadow, the moon slips.
Moon, moon – from you
measure, meter, memory, month.
The first calendar,
the first loss we saw coming.

Drowsing

Snow softens night,
heaps the bird house
like a lost pagoda.
Say blanket. Say
covering.

While the earth remains

While the earth remains, seedtime and harvest-time, cold and heat,
summer and winter, day and night, shall not cease.
                              — Genesis 8:22 (God's promise after the flood)

Let there always be taxol and chamomile,
abnormal pap smears and little shirts
with red snaps. Let there be trout with ginger
and green tea in the evenings.
Let there be months with nothing
but mac and cheese.
Let there be days when waking
is a heavy weight, a thickness
breathed in. Let there be weeks
together like this, weeks of sourness,
then one clean dawn in frost, the lawn smoking.
Let there be ticks in the saskatoons.
The one who picked saskatoons with me
one summer far from either of our lives
writes to say she cannot write or speak.
Let there be a lamp for her,
lasting oil, a little salt. Blessings.

Equinox today, the fall is coming.
Juniper dusty blue with berry, sumac
blushing. The tattered cherry
blooms again, a few bright blossoms.

Is that hope or hopelessness? The fruit
will never set. The flocks grow restless.
On this day the year is hinged
like a door. Let there always be
the gates of morning, the gates of evening.
Wheels. All creatures walking.

Let every thing take its right name:
rice and paper, salt and beans. Let dust
remember skin or desert, let the dust
film everything. Oh Lord, what comes
between us? Dust and thirst,
a lack of patience. Shyness.
There's skin at least, a secret
I don't know I'm keeping. What name
does it have? Shame. Eden.

While the earth remains, let there be spareness,
winter with one hawk and no hiding.
Let there be Junes jam-packed, chock-a-bloc, thick
with berries. Let all the graves have names.
Let us pray indifferently, pray in fear
and whispers, let us pray and be blasted
open. Let there be garlic and chilli,
and cream for the coffee, the salty
and sour, the sweet and the bitter, the desperate
and dappled, the morning
and evening, the over
and over, the first day.

Notes

Cover: The script below the icon reads "St. Mary Magdalene" in Syriac. In the Byzantine East, Christians remember that after the resurrection, Mary went to Rome, where she was accepted into the court of Caesar Tiberius. There, she used an egg to explain the resurrection, as later Patrick would use a shamrock to explain the trinity. On hearing her preach, Caesar exclaimed: "A man could no more rise from the dead than that egg could turn red." Of course, it promptly did.

How even the holy cover their faces: "You can't see why. You've just got to" is a quotation from Dianne Laney herself. The quotation beginning "If the ministry of death" is from 2 Corinthians 3, which is also where you'll find the title.

Leah names her sons: I am indebted to Robert Alter's translation of *Genesis* for explaining Leah's speeches of naming, and uncovering the Hebrew puns buried in, for instance, the name of her eldest Rueben: ru'ben means "see, a son."

"let my prayer be set forth in your sight...." The title is Ps 141:2 NKJV

"let us worship the Lord in the beauty of holiness..." The title is Ps 96:9. An alternate translation would make it "garments of holiness."

Job's plea: I was moved and informed by the translation and commentary by Raymond Scheindlin.

Chalcedony, crysoprase, lapis, onyx: The translations of the gemstone names from Rev 21 are doubtful. I took doubt as licence to play. I wrote this poem in Montreal at the League of Poets AGM, and it owes something to Anne Carson's keynote on the nature of dream.

Henini: the word Henini is a Hebrew exclamation of assent, usually translated as "Here I am."

I mention Robert Alter above. I am not a scholar, but he is. His many and masterful books of translation, commentary, and analysis have transformed and informed the Bible for me. This work would not be half what it is without his work to help me. If you find the Bible a closed door, a closed room, allow me to suggest reading Alter. For me, he opened locks, made scripture breathe.

Thanks

Some obligatory notes are nonetheless heart-felt. I thank the literary magazines in which some of these poems first appeared: *The New Quarterly, The Malahat Review, Prairie Fire, Event, Fiddlehead,* and *Descant.* And I thank the Ontario Arts Council, which supported this book through both the Works in Progress fund and the Writers' Reserve program. Readers and writing time – what better gifts are there?

I finished this manuscript during a residency at the Waterloo Public Library. The gig gave me endless coffee, a great big table, and – in my contact with community writers – near-daily reminders of how blessed a thing writing is. Cathy Matyas, the chief librarian at WPL, made this happen, as she does so much else in our town. Thank you, Cathy. Thank you, WPL!

In 2003, when I was a completely unknown (as opposed to mostly unknown) poet without even a first book, I was invited to read at the St. Jerome's Festival of Art and Spirit. It was Kim Jernigan – my dear friend, *New Quarterly* co-conspirator, and unofficial agent – who put a few poems under the nose of Michael Higgins, the President of St. Jerome's University, who responded with characteristic generosity. The reception I had at Arts and Spirit gave me early, vital energy.

At Art and Spirit I met Pier Giorgio DiCicco, whose poetry gave me courage and whose many letters gave me encouragement. It was he that shook me out of my smarminess and shame about religious writing. *Mille grazie,* George.

I thank the early readers who helped me bang together the structure of this manuscript: my mother in law Pat Bow, dear friend Marguerite Tonjes, sister Christian Lisa Inman, and sister poets Brianna Brash-Nyberg and Sharon Brogan. I also thank the Zeugma online workshop and the WELL poets and writers for their thoughtful readings of individual poems.

Finally, I thank the people who make so many books of Canadian poetry possible: Maria Jacobs and Noelle Allen of Wolsak and Wynn. They are generous, patient, keen, and talented – colleagues and friends.

There are a few poems I want to dedicate particularly: "As the fox-glove loves the fur of the bee" is for James Bow; "Yours is the day" is for Pier Giorgio DiCicco; "The kingdom of God is within you" is for Sharon Brogan; and "While the earth remains" is for Claudia Bickel. Bless you all.